Destined

WOMEN WITH VOICES FOR GOD

Destined: Women with Voices for God

© Copyright 2020 - All right reserved

The content contained within this book may not be reproduced, duplicated or transmitted without direct written permission from the author or the publisher.

Under non circumstances will any blame or legal responsibility be held against the publisher, or author, for any damages, reparation or monetary loss due to the information contained in this book, either directly or indirectly.

Legal notice: This book is copyright protected. It is only for personal use. You cannot amend, distribute, sell, use, quote or paraphrase any part or the content within this book without the authorization of the author or publisher.

All scripture references from NKJ and NIV Bibles.

Cover Design: Business Startup & Marketing Solutions LLC and JWG Publishing House.

For information regarding special discounts for bulk purchases of this book, for charitable donation, or speaking engagements, please visit: www.womenwithvoicesforgod.com or email obslconsultants@gmail.com

ISBN: 978-1-7339847-8-2
Published by JWG Publishing

Printed in the United States of America.

DEDICATION

This book is dedicated firstly to God, my Creator, who called me Destined before the foundations of this earth. I offer onto you Lord, the first fruits of this purpose. This book is also dedicated to my beloved father, the Reverend John F. Bell Sr. whom I love dearly. In addition, I dedicate this book to all the women with voices for God who have not yet answered the call of God upon their lives.

ACKNOWLEDGEMENTS

First, I would like to acknowledge Almighty God, who is the inspiration behind my entire life and the impetus of my purpose.

I would be remiss if I did not wholeheartedly acknowledge John Frank Bell Senior, my daddy, my guiding light. My relationship with God was fashioned from your relationship with God, and I thank you.

To my mother, Prophetess Mary Ann Miller, and my second dad, Minister Alvin Miller, thank you for your love and support and for standing by me. Mom, I love you. I watched you endure a lot over the years, and that has taught me to be resilient. You are destined for greatness and truly a remarkable woman. I want to thank you for being my mom and a preordained woman of God. I love you both.

To my wonderful, amazing and loving husband, Pastor Havard Lee Moton Sr., ten years ago while passing as strangers in church, I almost fell, and you caught me. You whispered in my ear "don't worry; I will never let you fall." Thank you for keeping your promise. I love you so much.

To my beloved children, Ashley, Shatira, Lavonte, Travonte, Zachary, and Jeremiah, and my awesome son-in-law Farel, you are all my pride and joy. Thank you for being my cheerleaders.

Shatira my quiet storm, you are always calm and always in charge; you are a leader whom God has called, and I am anticipating the moment at which you step into your purpose and fulfill your calling because you are truly destined for greatness.

To my lovely bonus sons and daughters whom I inherited through love: Matthew, Havard Junior, Lechelle, Dominique, Haywood, Shanarya, Shantoria, and Shantina and my wonderful daughter-in-law, Shannon; I love you all. My daughters, as you all continue to find yourselves in God, you will find your destined voices.

To my legacies, Za'Rhyia, Zy'Aire, Za'Rielle, Za'Relle, Lyrique, Lavonte Junior, Travonte Junior, and A'laijah, I am so blessed to witness your lives merging into mine. To my granddaughters, as you all continue to be nurtured by the Word of God, may your hearing be attuned to the voice of God, and bring forth your destined voices at His appointed time. Nana loves you all.

To my beloved brothers and sisters, Douglas, Sherlane, John Junior, Charles, David, and Denise, the first set of hearts that God entrusted me to care about, I love you all dearly. I would not trade any of you for the world. Sherlane, my almost twin and minister, our hearts are forever bound by the special childhood memories that we share. You are a great friend, sister, wife, and mother, whom God has chosen to speak on His behalf. Denise, my baby sister, you are a strong woman of God with a voice that the world is waiting to hear. You are a great wife and mother, and I am proud to call you baby sister. Walk into your destiny, I love you both.

To all my nieces, especially T'Ashia and Tierra, you are both young Esthers, called by God and ordained for a special time.

Walk as queens for the Kingdom of God. Hold your heads high and know that you are loved.

To my favorite and dearest uncle, Elder Lawrence Alston, I love you. You cared about us and protected us as your own while we were growing up. My childhood memories of you can never be erased.

To one of my co-authors and daughter, Prophetess Ashley, I am so proud of you for stepping out into this new role as an author and for walking in your purpose. You are an amazing mother, wife, and daughter. I love you. In addition, to my other co-authors, Pamela, Andrea, and Zakita, you are all destined women who have recognized your voices that you have each chosen to use for God. I applaud your courage and tenacity in pushing through to the finish line. I love you all.

To Changing Lives Ministries and Deliverance Center, my beloved church family, thank you for all the love and support with which you shower me each Sunday. I appreciate your prayers. They are never too much. I love you all.

To my Minister, friend, and fellow author Marcia, you are an incredible woman of God whom I have had the privilege to watch God use mightily. I have seen your spiritual growth and faith bloom. Thank you for your support and encouragement and for allowing me to humbly guide you. I love you. You are truly destined.

To my friends, Susana, Sandra, Cheryl, Lacretia, and Stephanie, thank you all for your genuine friendships and your sisterly support throughout the years. I love you all so much.

To my spiritual parents, Bishop Ervin Clay III and Prophetess Sheila Clay, thank you both for your heartfelt love and support. I really appreciate your unwavering support as Havard and I stepped into our ministry, and now into new areas of our calling. Thank you and I love you both dearly.

To my eight-hour-a-day family, my co-workers, and fellow therapists, thank you for your daily encouragement while writing this book. You all have been incredibly supportive. Thank you all. Aleida, I call you my work mom. We share a special mother-daughter bond. God loves you dearly, and you are very special to Him, and me. Thank you for always feeding me and taking care of me.

Kristina, my awesome supervisor, you are always encouraging me. Thank you for your constant positivity toward me. You are a gifted woman who is destined for higher heights in God. To Natalie, you are truly sent from God. You have blessed my life more than you will ever know. I admire your walk with Christ and the woman of God you are. To Carolyn, thank you so much, for your encouraging words and support, I truly appreciate you. God cares for you so much. I love you all.

To Crystal, a special friend who I met whilst we were both at a place of healing, you are one of the great inspirations that have given me the courage to encourage other destined voices like yourself. You are a remarkable woman who is very special to God. You have truly touched my life. Thank you.

To my publisher, Joan Wright-Good, and her awesome winning team, I came to you because God led me to you. You are blessed with the gift of interpreting a vision given by God and bringing it to life as He did with mine. You are a destined woman with a gift of birthing other women into their destiny. Thank you for your support and for believing in my debut project. Thank you for pushing me beyond my limits. You have encouraged me beyond measure.

Contents

Introduction 1

CHAPTER 1: *Recognizing the Call* 5

CHAPTER 2: *The Purpose of The Call* 15

CHAPTER 3: *Birthing of The Purpose* 19

CHAPTER 4: *Walking in The Purpose* 23

CHAPTER 5: *Destiny Is Not A Position; It Is A Journey* 29

CHAPTER 6: *God Wants Us to Be Unstuck* 41

CHAPTER 7: *Chosen for Destiny* 45

CHAPTER 8: *Get Back in The Game* 47

CHAPTER 9: *Liberation* 53

The Power of Words for The Destined Woman 53

CHAPTER 10: *Sis Accept Who You Are!* 75

INTRODUCTION

Destined: Women with Voices for God was inspired solely by the Holy Spirit. While I was driving alone in my car on my way to Bible study one summer evening, the Holy Spirit impressed upon me the name 'Women with Voices.' Along with the name 'Women with Voices,' the Holy Spirit also downloaded various facets to this idea by giving me detailed instructions on how to bring this plan to life. The voice of God also insisted on the urgency to get this plan moving right away. As some of you are aware, when God drops an idea or plan into your hands, you may only receive one line of instructions, and it is usually in an area within which you have no expertise and must therefore depend solely on His word-by-word instructions. I began to make inquiries and stumbled upon the first roadblock. The name Women with Voices was already legally taken. I paused for a moment and then the suggestion was made to add 'for God' to the name, hence the name Women with Voices for God (WWVG). Guess what? That name was not taken by anyone so now it belongs to me.

This first book Destined aims to elaborate on one of several specific attributes descriptive of women set apart and divinely appointed to become Women with Voices for God. As such, the term 'destined' will be a recurring theme that describes the trajectory of ordinary women doing extraordinary things for God through the use of their collective voices within spiritual realms. When I began writing this book, as the Lord further instructed me to do, I was transported to my early years as a child when the Lord touched my heart and activated my childlike faith in Him. My father knew that God had placed a special calling on my life, so even at a young age, I was aware of a special connection between God and myself. I could not put my finger on it to describe exactly what it was, but I knew that there was a very special connection, that always drew me to God. I had a desire and a yearning for God, even as a child. As I got older and started walking in my purpose, God gave me these words to describe the purpose, 'Women with Voices for God.'

The word destined is defined by the Oxford Dictionary as being developed according to a specific plan. It implies being consistently developed, equipped and shaped, to eventually achieve the highest levels of accomplishments and pre-determined purpose. Before sin entered into the Garden of Eden and interrupted the perfect plan that God established for humanity, there was no need to tell Adam and Eve that they were since they were already living and enjoying the benefits of creation according to God's plans. However, when sin entered, God's perfect plan was tainted, and as a result, man fell from God's grace. God, through His mercy and love for His creation, established a plan to return humanity to its original state. Just like Adam and Eve, when we inevitably fall prey to a sinful state, we become sidetracked and stray away from God's plans for our lives. The compounded adversarial issues that we face in our own lives distract us. I have come across so many persons, especially women like myself, who, at one point, were so lost in life that they had forgotten (or may not have even been aware), that God had a plan for their lives.

There are several examples in the Bible of women who were predestined by God with a set plan for their lives before they came into existence. Ruth, Esther, Deborah, Rahab, Hannah, and Mary, mother of Jesus, just to name a few. Initially destined toward becoming a voice for God, at some point in their early lives, each woman endured challenging circumstances that appeared to still their voices.

God has used Women with Voices for God to identify women who are destined for greatness and service. This concept provides clarity to women in their quest for a deeper understanding of the call on their lives, and the ability to recognize that such a call was preordained and uniquely patterned for each of them. It is my prayer and hope that my sisters from all walks of life, all races and nations, will hear the voice of God, and be reminded that despite the challenges and obstacles that may have led them astray, there is a predestined voice placed inside of them that God is still longing to hear. I encourage you, my reader, to always remember that YOU ARE DESTINED.

CHAPTER 1

Recognizing the Call

Tara Moton

Sheltered:

We were all very sheltered. That is the best way I can describe growing up, being raised in a strict, yet loving household, where my 6ft 3in father powerfully and prophetically preached the Word of God while my mother balanced ministry and family. Strong Christian Southern principles practiced amongst my five siblings, were influenced by my  father, who was born and raised in Buena Vista, Georgia, and my mother who hailed from Charleston, South Carolina. Destiny brought their paths together in South Florida where they got married. We did everything together as a family: going to church, taking trips, and going fishing. Friday nights were extra special because that was the evening when dad would bring home seafood that we all loved. We would have a slumber party in the living room where we ate seafood and watched our favorite television shows such as 'Dallas' and 'The Dukes of Hazzard'. This was the one time each week when our parents allowed us to watch television. They purposely protected us from the secular world by sheltering us from the outside influences of secular music and worldly lifestyles. Schoolwork and Christian principles prevailed.

Being the eldest, I always had a sense of responsibility for my younger siblings. My mother Mary always said I had a very mature disposition, just like a little lady. While other little girls were playing with dolls or having fun outdoors, I was seriously contemplating how I was going to help Jesus save the world. The worldview of my surrounding environment, both inside and outside of my home, was very different. As I grew older, I quietly observed how people interacted with each other and how they lived. While I could see their natural lives with my physical eyes, God would reveal the hidden parts of their inner lives that could only be seen through the workings of the Spirit. He would open up their hearts, their hurts, their expectations, and even sometimes their darkest secrets, and give me an overview of their lives. I always felt different around my classmates at school.

I knew they all thought I was weird. As a first grader, I was always armed with my tightly clutched Holy Bible which I considered to be my Super Girl weapon; it became the means by which I would prophesy to the other first graders. I thought I was fine. I also had dolls that I played with at home. I would dress them up, while pretending to be my mother in church; I could always be found preaching and prophesying to them in my bedroom. I was often isolated and not included in groups or cliques at school. That isolation worsened when the things that I spoke about were confirmed. Destined individuals are often isolated because they are misunderstood. They communicate at a higher level with God, and as the Bible says, "the natural man cannot understand the things of the Spirit," 1 Corinthians 2:14.

I knew God spoke to me just as He spoke through my daddy, and watching my father preach and prophesy only strengthened my desire to become a true servant of God. Maybe this was how the Prophet Samuel felt as a child as he heard the voice of God, recognized the voice of God, and most importantly, obeyed the voice of God. Now when I think about it, my father was also like Eli, the priest whom God entrusted to bridle the young prophet's life. My dad and I used to share many deep conversations where he taught me so much about the Almighty God and his trusted source. As a young child, I would often experience the supernatural movement of the Holy Spirit and was amazed and curious at the power that exuded through worship. I witnessed infirmed people being healed miraculously and saw issues that the average child could not comprehend.

In my eyes, my dad was a giant in physical stature, and a giant in ministry. I remember how much I revered my father's connection with God. I felt as though he could reach up and grasp hold of God's hand and they would begin to commune. One day my dad suddenly went blind for 3 days. I was frightened because he could not see, and I was worried that he would hurt himself trying to move around. He was never a lazy person to sit around;

he always had to be on the move. After all, we were a household of five energetic children. As I stared at my father one day, who could not see the tears in my eyes, I watched him with his head gently resting back on the sofa as if he was resting in the arms of Jesus, and he began to worship God. Even as I write, I am crying profusely because I have been transported back to that specific moment when I was exceptionally privileged to share with my father the true essence of a powerful worship experience.

During the three-day period of his vision, loss my dad would ask me to read the Bible to him and would have me lay my hands on his eyes to pray for his healing. My faith was strong because I wanted my dad to regain his sight. I believed and knew that God would deliver him. I remember it as if it happened yesterday; putting my hands over my dad's eyes and praying. Once the prayer was over, my dad would rest his head backward for a little while. I made sure I remained very close to him at all times because in my little heart I knew, without a doubt, that God would heal my precious dad, and I did not want to miss that divine moment.

My anxious heart loved God, even more, when He did it! He healed my dad. My sturdy and humbled father stood up without saying a word and opened his blinded eyes. His sight returned, just like the blind man who Jesus healed with clay and saliva. Dad looked at me and he saw me. At that moment, I was amazed. My mom, overhearing me asking my dad if he could see me, hurried in from the kitchen. We all praised God as my dad walked around the house. At eight years old, little did I know that my father's actions were planting the seeds that would take root, to bear the foundation of my calling.

He was my greatest childhood influence and the one who was responsible for giving me some early insight into my strangely unique experiences. He not only gave me clarity, but also gave me a sense of confidence as only a true father could give to his precious daughter. We had many great talks and we talked about everything. My curious mind had so many questions about God that only he could answer. My father was my gateway to God. I admired this man so much for his humility, his wisdom, his profound attentiveness to my mom, and his unwavering and unfathomable love for his children. I now comprehend what it means to exhibit a Godly character because my father portrayed what it meant to cultivate a close relationship with our heavenly Father, not only with words but also by deeds. I was always intrigued by how he interacted with the Lord as if He was his best friend. I wanted to be a friend of God as well. I wanted God to use me in the same manner that He used my dad and to make the world a better place. I literally wanted to be Super Girl for Jesus, and constantly walked around clutching my Bible as my shield. I knew it protected me, and I knew that there was power in it.

I was not as versed in scripture, compared to my dad, but I knew in my heart that there was a protective element that the Holy Bible provided, and I was so confident and secure in my faith in its promises that I held onto it dearly. As I reflect on it now, and according to Ephesians 6:16 where it speaks about the shield of faith being a crucial piece of armor, it all made sense that I would walk around with my physical Bible to protect me from the darts that the enemy was forming to attack my life. As my destined life traveled through various dark valleys, later on, my shield of faith, which is the word of God, was the only armor that held me together and protected my mind from mental disintegration.

As far back as when I was two years old, I remember some of my relatives and family friends who would gamble a lot, and play the numbers game, or as they called it, night house and cubic. They would come over to our house and secretly ask me, "Lady," as I was called, "give me the numbers", and I would innocently report the numbers that appeared in my head. The numbers were correct as my uncles and other family members always returned to our house extra happy and seeking more predictions. In my innocence, I did not know that I was being spiritually exploited, but once my father found out, he ended this practice. He recognized the gift of prophecy that enveloped my life from birth and did his best to protect me and taught me that this gift is to be used to make people's lives better and to glorify God. Spiritual exploitation is sadly a common experience of destined people. As a pastor and professional therapist, one of my most common observations through counseling clients as well as my personal experience is that I find there is a deep-rooted correlation between spiritual exploitation and sexual exploitation, where the latter oftentimes follows the former.

When you are destined for a specific purpose, it does not begin once you give your life to Christ and confess your sins to Him. He is your Lord and Savior. It does not start when you attain adulthood; it does not even commence when you think you are ready to accept your calling. According to the conversation in Jeremiah 1:5, God informs a youthful inexperienced Jeremiah "I knew you before I formed you in the womb; I set you apart for me before you were born; I appointed you to be a prophet to the nations." For destined individuals, our lives are no different than that of the prophet Jeremiah. Our blueprints are all the same, divinely created by God long before we were formed in our mothers' wombs. My dad always knew ever since my birth and told me that God had chosen and anointed me for a greater purpose. I adored my father even more so because he was my spiritual, religious, and social mentor.

I watched the way God would use him, how he exercised a unique approach to preaching, and the many lives that were impacted because of how he completely allowed the Holy Spirit to use him in such a selfless way. I have always had the understanding that my father was just an ordinary man, but once the Holy Spirit took charge of his mortal body, he was able to accomplish extraordinary things. I recognized that it was God who was in control and directed his every move and every spoken word. And as it was then, so it is now with me. As a pastor and prophetess, having had that understanding rooted within me from an early age, it has kept me spiritually cognizant of the fact that I am just a tool through which God chooses to use and operate. I am fully aware that if God does not speak through me, or if He does not reveal to me, and if I do not hear His voice, then I am only operating in my human capacity. Therefore, I must not move without His divine instructions or directions.

Destined individuals should not entertain disobedience in their lives, whether on purpose or by default. It is easier for a regular sinner to find temporary ways to escape the consequences of sin from disobedience. However, for a destined individual who is aware of the ordained calling on his or her life, there is no escaping the consequences of their disobedient actions, but to face the Caller of their destiny. Whether the destined person disobeyed on purpose or by default, they are still held accountable by God. The scripture warns us in 1st Samuel chapter 15 vs 22, that while a sacrificial offering is good for the redemption of a disobedient or sinful way, God is more pleased when obedience is followed without resistance. It is better to obey than having to create a sacrificial offering. You do not know if God will even accept your sacrificial offering, so it is better to obey than not. Our Father knows us and knows exactly for what specific purpose He has set us apart. God calls us first by awakening our spiritual awareness of His presence hovering over us. He begins to draw us by impressing upon our minds the necessity for training our thoughts on Him.

You will find yourself strangely thinking outside of your normal thinking pattern. Things that make you go "hmmm, I never thought of that before." We don't know how that call will come. For Samuel, it was an unfamiliar voice at first. For Joseph, his call came in the form of dreams. For Moses, he never heard a voice at first, but he saw an anomaly; a burning bush that was not burning. The sight of the burning bush stopped him in his tracks, then the voice of the Lord spoke. In whatever way or form the call comes, God first halts your movement; He gets your attention; and then He speaks.

God is a God of order; He doesn't join the circus or the noise. How did God stop you in your tracks? How has God gotten your attention? Or, is He still waiting for you to answer? It is okay if you hear Him, even if you may not know why. However, once you hear

His voice or see His deliberate signs, just answer. God never gives us the full picture of His plan for our call. Abraham did not know the scope of the plans that God had for his life, but he simply obeyed. Joseph did not know the depths of his call, and I am quite sure he became more confused when his brothers sold him into slavery, but he still obeyed the call by keeping his faith in God.

Then there is David who kept his faith in God and answered even when faced with oppression from King Saul. He knew he was anointed to sit on the throne over Israel despite potential conflict; the mighty King Saul was still reigning when God called an inexperienced David from his sheep-keeping duties to take up the mantle. David is a great example of someone who was destined.

CHAPTER 2

The Purpose of The Call

The call on one's life precedes the purpose of the call. If God is calling you or seeking your attention, there is a good reason behind it. Just brace yourself, because attempting to explain the reason of such a call, may well be futile. God is the only one who uses you and then restores you. On the other hand, when someone uses you and utilizes your most valuable assets for selfish benefits, they take the best of you.

Your gifts and talents can be manipulated or exploited, leaving you dry, desolate, and broken. When a man cannot harvest any further resources from an individual, they can, without conscience, discard the person aside like trash. In other words, they may see you as valueless and disposable. Some employers and many corporate-based organizations employ this practice frequently because it tends to follow the guidelines of several business models. What is the sense in keeping something that is no longer of value to them? If it doesn't benefit them anymore, why keep it? If you interview a few individuals who were the victims of wrongful termination from their jobs, I am positive that you will hear similar stories of individuals who invested extensive and dedicated service to an organization but failed to receive significant assistance from their employer after an illness or family crisis. There are workers who were denied opportunities for promotions, pay raises, and health benefits only as a result of ageism – a discriminatory practice; there are frequent instances in which some employees might have been laid off or terminated based on unsubstantiated claims of 'poor job performance' by a supervisor, when the actual reason might have been age discrimination.

It is only God who will call you and utilize your life on earth for His glory while He simultaneously restores you. If you dedicate your gifts, talents, and your spiritual and earthly service to the Great One who has preordained you before you were formed in the womb, you can guarantee that your life will experience the abundant living that God already promised to you. God is the only employer who can guarantee everlasting benefits; His insurance policy is eternally guaranteed, and it never expires. His guarantee is found in His word. Who would not want to work for Him or serve Him?

There is nothing that God does that is simple. Everything that

He performs is great. Even the simplest pleasures of nature that we enjoy are great works at the hands of God. Whatever the purpose that God has called you for, it is great. He will work great things through you, but you should always remember that the call is given to initiate the purpose of your destiny. Just as how electricity flows through its conduit, the conduit is only the carrier for power. The conduit is not great, it is only the power flowing through it, that is great. Being destined does not mean that you are the great one; however, the work that is associated with the call that has been entrusted to you, is great. You are destined to accomplish great things for the service of the Lord.

When you are destined, you must remember to remain humble because if you do not, deception enters the heart, and the risk of believing that you are omnipotent will definitely halt your trajectory towards your destined path to greatness. The loss of humility gives way to self-centeredness which then leads to the displacement of the One who should always be the center of our lives, and the giver of abundant life. We frequently observe so-called religious persons who brag and advertise about their perceived infinite power and wealth. "Look at what I am doing! Look at me and what God gave me, my new house, and my new car." Who benefits from all the self-boasting and self-glorification? It is certainly not God, but only the boaster. Is God being glorified? He is not. How is your boasting helping to change someone's life or putting him or her in the right direction?

When you are destined, it does not just affect your life, it is not just for you. God's investment in you does not work like that. Those who are destined affect hundreds, thousands, millions, cities, nations, and even the world. Your being destined is not just for you but it's for others and also for those whom you have never met. If you remain humble, God will place the spotlight on you, the one who has been designated to be His chosen vessel; He will show you off, and no one but God can be ascribed that credit, because He is the great one in you.

CHAPTER 3

Birthing of The Purpose

———⸙☙⸙———

Birthing of your destiny is much like the natural birthing of a child except that it happens in different realms. The birthing of a baby takes place in the physical womb of the woman with the separation of the pelvic region to deliver the living baby. The birthing of your destiny happens through the realm of the Spirit where the pain is manifested through the difficult circumstances that surround the birthing of your destiny. The birth of your destiny is never pain-free. Issues will arise from all angles - in your personal life and on your job; and issues can arise from anywhere. For most women who have had the opportunity to give birth, it can be a beautiful and wonderful experience. From conception through the trimesters, the experience is like no other, and I am sure that we can all agree on that point.

In the early stages of most pregnancies, nausea is usually the first indicator in most cases of a suspected pregnancy. As the pregnancy develops, the nausea increases, and the woman's body goes through increased cycles of discomfort and uneasiness. By the time the ninth month arrives, the mother is feeling all the pressure of the full baby exerting pressure on the base of her uterus.

Both mother and child have similar goals. The baby is saying, "I need to get out of here, I can't fit, it's too small in here!" While on the outside, the mother is pleading with God to bring the labor on, at whatever cost, because she must get this thing out of her. Labor is the most difficult part of every pregnancy. It is the beginning of the delicate birthing process where life and death travel the same road for both mother and unborn baby. Labor pain, in its full force, is excruciating, unbearable and is incomparable.

The spiritual birthing of your destiny also comes with spiritual pain. While we are being processed to fulfill the purpose of our destiny, our lives go through changes and transformations, which are only accomplished through the Holy Spirit. Similarly, also, as the mother's physical body experiences changes during her growing pregnancy, our spiritual characters also undergo transformations that cannot be seen with the natural eyes, during the processing of our destinies. God wants us to think and speak like Him. He wants us to carry His heart. All of those changes take place in our lives to promote the great purpose that is getting ready to be born through us. The mother's body must change to

BIRTHING OF THE PURPOSE

accommodate the growing baby. Not all pregnant women carry the beautiful 'pregnancy glow.' Frankly, some women experience horrible changes in their skin texture, visible permanent stretch marks, and some even experience hair loss. The calcium that the baby extracts from the mother can affect her hair, bones and teeth.

Despite the external physical appearance of the mother, the baby on the inside is protected. During our spiritual processes, our lives may not be so appealing to others because of the spiritual battles that we face. It may appear as if everything is going wrong in our lives. Regardless of being protected and unexposed to physical touch, the birth of our purpose must take place. The word of God says, "So shall my Word be that goes forth out of my mouth; It shall not return unto me void, but it shall accomplish that which I please, and it shall prosper in the thing whereto I sent it" Isaiah 55:11. Therefore, destined reader, a word to you is that if God has stopped you in your tracks, and has spoken to you about a purpose, rest assured, according to this scripture, that the birthing of your purpose must take place.

I have experienced both types of birthing which I have discussed so far. My last physical pregnancy was one of the most impactful deliveries in my life; in the labor room, it felt as if I was giving birth, physically and spiritually. I was aware of my spiritual calling and this pregnancy with my son eighteen years ago came when God had processed me, and I was about to give birth to the purpose of my destiny.

My marriage, at the time, was unstable, volatile, and unpredictable. I had to deal with a physical, growing pregnancy and spiritual processing at the same time, both manifesting changes in my entire life. I was happy about my baby that was coming and looking forward to his birth. However, while I was happy about my new baby, my life was in turmoil. The enemy tried to destroy my mind by plunging me into a state of total depression. I knew that I had to stay balanced in my mental faculties for the sake of my other children and my unborn child. The one thing that kept me together was the same thing that kept me together as a child - dealing with my dad's disease, and my daily attachment to my Bible. I held onto my Bible throughout the entire nine months of my pregnancy. I isolated myself from others, and experienced passive suicidal ideations while my mental stability declined.

By the time the baby was ready to be born, I was hospitalized for over a month due to severe hemorrhaging. As I was being rushed into surgery due to the baby being in distress, I clutched my Bible even more tightly as I felt my spirit walking away from my bulging body. At that moment, as surgery was being performed on me to save the life of my unborn baby, the Spirit of the Lord met with me. It appeared that for an extended period of time, I was walking with the Lord on this beautiful gold paved road; He showed me beautiful scenes that came into view on my left and right. I was left with an enveloping feeling of euphoria. The conversation was peaceful with God, and as I moved to go forward with Him, he stopped me and said "It is not your time. I have great work for you to do." As my body physically gave birth to my son, the Holy Spirit delivered me into my purpose.

CHAPTER 4

Walking in The Purpose

―――――― ⁀ᩛ⌒ ――――――

Eighteen years later, and now as a pastor and professional therapist, the Lord has purposed me to help persons who are destined to recognize the call on their life. Whether they are church members, clients, or co-workers, I have come across destined individuals who are unaware of the spiritual calling on their lives but are puzzled by the different circumstances in which God is trying to get their attention. Most of the time, they associate it with the natural aspects of life, being unable to recognize their calling due to a lack of spiritual insight and awareness.

God has also blessed me with the ability to differentiate between a spiritual calling and a natural mental disorder. Medically speaking, many medical professionals operate solely through science. Their diagnosis and treatment are strictly within the confines of medicine. For example, if the young prophet Samuel was living in the present-day 21st century and reported to his teacher that he is hearing a voice calling to him during his bedtime, the teacher would most certainly report it. He would have been sent to the school counselor, and his parents notified and informed that he must be assessed by a child psychiatrist. While it is true that he heard a voice, in present-day customs, Samuel would have been misdiagnosed, negatively labeled, and ultimately deterred from his calling.

I am not trying to distract from the realities of mental disorders. It is however important that the assessor is able to discern the difference between genuine mental disorder and a spiritual encounter with God.

Today, my insight and ability to discern more clearly the revelation of why the Lord, since year 2000, sternly instructed me to enter into the field of studies for mental health, have come into perfect view. Having also experienced severe depression and passive suicidal ideation in my own life, the Lord wanted me to have a broader knowledge about mental health in general, how it is treated medically, and how to incorporate the skills to spiritually distinguish other causes that impact a person's psychosocial and spiritual condition. Prior to each counseling session, I seek the Lord for His divine supervision over the session. As I listen keenly to each client speaking, the Lord will reveal key information about the client, while I wait for confirmation of words from the person. For example, the client may be sharing something traumatic from their childhood or past, and the Holy Spirit will confirm and reveal even more hidden issues. This double-layered set of information gives me a wider understanding and observation of the clients' level of stability.

Spiritual Health:

Spiritual, mental, emotional, and physical health are very important as these four components create balance for an individual's life. I define spiritual health as a conscious awareness of our Creator who is a spiritual being; it is recognizing that we are also spiritual beings that exist in physical and temporal bodies.

According to the word of God, we were created long before we became beings in the form of flesh. Again, God confirmed to Jeremiah that He knew him before he was flesh in his mother's womb. This tells me that if God says He knew us before we were in flesh form, He had to have known us in the Spirit. God is a Spirit and a Spirit only. If we understand that concept, it will lead us to our identity, and we can only find our identities in God. It is like returning to our place of birth where we can access all the information about our birthing.

People who are adopted or given up at birth usually struggle with finding their identity. They want to know who they resemble; from whom they inherit certain genetic traits and how such traits may inform their overall heritage. More frequently, they undergo years of tedious and costly searches, merely to discover who they are. When we understand who we are, it creates a solid structure on which our lives can stand and grow.

Emotional Health:

Having the capability to control one's response in reacting to negative issues that may affect thoughts, feelings, and behaviors, is what I consider to be the foundation of excellent emotional health. Much of our daily news broadcasts significantly contribute to the over-abundance of poor emotional health frequently observed in many of our homes, schools, communities, and our nation at large.

Mass shootings that occur too often in our nation are usually the result of individuals who cannot control their emotions, especially the emotion of anger. Humans experience a flood of emotions naturally, but most are still able to utilize practical coping skills that will allow them to control their emotional reactions in diverse situations, and not allow a negative reaction to replace a sound decision. We sadly see suicide and murders being the tragic outcome of severed love relationships, with one or both parties being unable to emotionally withstand the hurtful feelings of being rejected. Bullying is another prime example of individuals who are suffering from inferior emotional thoughts and feelings, which may be manifested through their negative and manipulative abuse of others, resulting in emotional and more frequently, physical harm.

Mental Health:

Mental health and emotional health walk hand in hand. If spiritual, emotional, and physical health are not in place in one's life, it follows that there is the greater potential for deterioration in their overall wellbeing and mental health.

Physical Health:

Physical health comprises physical fitness, a balanced diet, and regular medical checkups. It is always encouraging to develop some kind of activity that gets your body moving, whether it is dancing, swimming, playing sports, or exercising. It has been proven that exercising can contribute to the betterment of your emotional and mental well- being. Exercising can also help eliminate stress, anxiety, aggressiveness, and improve one's mood. Children also experience a variety of emotions and need a positive outlet, and sporting activities are usually highly recommended to counter this problem.

I would recommend that a destined individual not only take charge of their spiritual health but also include all four components. A person who is destined must be acutely aware of their identity and must be well balanced. You must try to maintain good health practices as it is vital and requires discipline. Destined individuals MUST embody the discipline of Christ. It will not happen overnight, but obedience will allow you to become disciplined.

CHAPTER 5

Destiny Is Not A Position; It Is A Journey

Zakita Fulmore

If you had asked me where I was going in life and what I wanted to be, a Mental Health Therapist would not have even crossed my mind. Allow me to take you on a short journey as to how I got to this place in my life. Experiencing challenges of my own as a single parent took me in a different direction in life. I decided to return to school in 2015, to further my education in graduate school. At the time, I was headstrong on becoming a police officer, so I studied Criminal Justice with a concentration in Behavioral Science. This was more than a Master of Science degree for me; it was first, a peek into a better understanding of why people commit crimes and then to gain a better understanding of why and how individuals act in certain ways.

The second part is, it helped me to understand behavior in others and led me to help people manage their behaviors and impulses. The same year I began graduate school was the same year I began teaching. The first class of students I taught was all third-grade boys. Whew, did they have a hard time for the first few weeks! However, I gained authority and control of my classroom as time went by. This was my first-time correlating behavior with my graduate studies. I can recall at a very young age, during my elementary years that children close to my age and a little older always felt comfortable coming to me to talk about their problems. They would confide in me about circumstances that created severe challenges.

I did not realize it then, but I have always had a kind heart, offered sound advice, and could provide guidance to those in need. At that time, I did not understand what God was doing in my life. I have always had compassion for others and their well-being. As I got older, I became wiser while my walk with God grew stronger. On beginning my career path, children with challenging behaviors were mainly sent to me because I could handle it. At times, I was able to connect to those children beyond the classroom; I developed the skill of identifying and soothing the place in their hearts that hurt the most. Once I was able to make that connection and the child knew that I cared, their behavior improved, and their learning gains increased. As a Mental Health Therapist, my heart's desire is to help those that are hurting and in need of guidance. So, when I got my first class after Graduate school and I realized that the group of students I taught, mostly came from broken homes, and had issues such as: being children of divorced or single parents, facing challenges such as malnourishment, financial instability, limited resources, and being victims and/or witnesses to domestic violence, I knew that it was time for ministry.

As I learned the background history of my students, I was able to reach them in more unique ways. I also learned that in teaching, I should become more aware that all students are unique and should not be grouped as having similar needs. My heart went out to these students because I knew they did not have a choice regarding the direction in which their lives were going. Knowing all this, it drew me in even more and made me feel true compassion for these children. At the same time, I obtained a better perception of motherhood and the situation going on with my child. As I was reaching out to help my students, my personal life began spiraling out of control. My daughter was 4 years old in VPK and her temper, anger, and aggression increased more and more, to the point where I was beginning to get phone calls at work, because, my daughter was tearing the school to pieces. Her tantrums included throwing chairs, desks, books, and bookshelves. She would also scream and run out of the classroom and the building.

For the life of me, I could not understand her level of defiance and rage. I sought help when I realized my tactics of discipline and mother-daughter talks weren't enough. I went to doctors who told me initially, that it was too early to diagnose her with a particular disorder but would still prescribe for her a low dosage medication geared toward calming her down. It did not work; instead, it made her more aggressive.

Moving on to her kindergarten school year, at the same private Christian school, things went further downhill. I looked into getting her a therapist, but that did not work either. My daughter became attached to the therapist and began to use that as a form of manipulation to get out of doing her schoolwork. Learning was not the problem; her teacher would tell me that my daughter would correctly complete her assignment within two to three minutes. However, she displayed an inability to sit and remain in class and be compliant with her teachers.

It came to the point where the school Director was calling me to leave work to pick up my child daily, which eventually led to them indirectly kicking her out of the school. By this time, I was working at a charter school, teaching fourth grade. I was barely hanging on by a thread. I was broken, frustrated, and an emotional wreck. Somehow, by the grace of God, I was still holding on. I will be honest, there were times when I wanted to give up, but I knew that if I gave up, I would have no one to fight for my child. I therefore decided to enroll my daughter in the school where I was working, thinking I would have a better handle and an advantage with her being at the same place I was. It was rough in the beginning. The first few days, she was running out of class, yelling, and throwing things. I was embarrassed and worn-out. The staff was helpful and kind in the beginning. The teacher formulated a plan to reward my daughter when she did good things. This plan worked for about three weeks and then the teacher got tired and sloppy and stopped following through on the behavior treatment. Keep in mind that I am still attending school, teaching a class of twenty-nine, and helping students make learning gains in the midst of all this.

I soon learned that the teacher was taunting my daughter by doing things that increased her anger, such as excluding her from activities, and recording her behavior without my permission or consent. Staff began talking behind my back and things turned bitter and sour quickly. I snatched my daughter from school so fast; no one knew until her new school called requesting her transcripts. It was around this time I began to understand that my daughter's behavior was not something just in the natural, but a spiritual attack designed to destroy me and take me out. Unbelievably, I had not reached my breaking point, but it was soon underway.

I enrolled my daughter at a public school near home. In the beginning, I thought she was doing well because I was not getting any phone calls. After two weeks, sure enough, they began rolling in. After a few months, I resigned from teaching and went into the legal field and obtained a career as a paralegal. On my lunch breaks, I began going out to my daughter's school periodically, to check on her. The number of parent conferences I attended and the many write-ups and suspensions they had my daughter's name on, made her look like a monster on paper. How I made it through her kindergarten year, was only God.

The thing about my daughter is that she was selective with her behavior. There were age-appropriate issues at home, nothing extreme, but at school, where she was so misunderstood, is where

I noticed things escalated and got out of control quickly. Around this time, I had another therapist that gave up on my child and a psychiatrist too. The psychiatrist told me he did not feel like he was helping my daughter and said there was nothing further he could do. Now, I am thinking to myself, "Lord, why does everyone keep giving up on my child? Why is this so hard?" This was my breaking point. I recognized that I had been in spiritual warfare and did not even realize it. I realized I was not equipped to handle this naturally. I told myself, "you've tried the teachers and doctors with failed responses; it is time to try God." So, I took my trust out of men and put all my faith in God.

In the summer of 2017, I began attending church. Now, I grew up in church and the thing is, I knew better. But I thought I could, and I had to handle this all by myself, but I heard God say, "the battle is not yours." When I came to God, I was broken, depressed, and oh, I was so depressed. I had developed anxiety and my anxiety came from the excessive worry I endured with my daughter. On the first Sunday, I attended church. I went to the altar, and I broke down. I felt the mothers of the church surrounding me and immediately began praying for me. I felt them rubbing my back and I knew in the Spirit it was because of all that I had been going through. I was so desperate for God to change my circumstances. I did not care who was looking at me because only I knew how much I suffered; the fact is I nearly lost my mind but didn't; I knew God had a purpose for me.

The second Sunday I attended the same church and went to the altar again where the First Lady prophesied to me. She told me, I would be a leading and guiding light to many young women that would flock to me for strength. I listened and received the Word of God, but I did not understand it as I was still working at the law firm. I continued going to church while I developed my relationship with God. I began to understand that only God could get me through this. I came to a place where God showed me that I had to be in the right place and remain aligned with God in order to see a change in my daughter.

As summer 2017 ended and the new school year was fast approaching, I withdrew my daughter from the school she was attending and moved her to a school in Miami. On the first day, my daughter's tantrums returned, and she resorted to her old familiar behaviors. The calls started again. I was still going to church, trusting the will of God, and getting prayer for my daughter, as well as for myself. With consistency, time, and prayer, I began to see improvement with my daughter's behavior. She was staying in class, doing her work, and making gradual progress. Shortly thereafter, the enemy sent another form of attack. Boys began bullying my daughter. She would tell me about it and tell the teacher and, in the beginning, something was being done about it. Later, many changes came into play.

My daughter does not respond well to rapid change and transition. The third teacher with whom she was placed, went on leave, so there were numerous substitutes. The bullying and taunting increased, but this time, it was evident that no one in administration made an effort to correct the situation. I went out to the school to find out what was going on, and of course, my child was continually being blamed. My daughter began to get slammed on the ground by boys; at times she was pushed, punched, and scratched in her face. How could my daughter be blamed for this? Soon, my daughter reverted to her defiant behaviors and went into survival mode. She stopped listening, ran around the school, engaged in fighting, and was back to throwing chairs, desk, and whatever she could put her hands on.

In March 2018, I began teaching Adult Education. The day I began in this position, all hell broke loose. From the day I started this job until June of that year, I went out to my daughter's school every single day! I was called at least three times a day. At this job, I was thriving and was informed that I was making astronomical gains and meeting goals they had never seen with students. My career was taking off, but I felt like my personal life was deteriorating. I asked myself that if I did not advocate for my child, who would?

I began to see that the word which was prophesied to me nearly a year ago, came to pass in significant and noticeable ways. I started to understand that I was approaching my destiny and the enemy was in full attack mode. I tell you, only God kept me. Towards the end of the school year, my pastor told me about a new Christian private school that would help my daughter tremendously. He told me she needed to be in the right place with the right people. He told me that when people did not understand an individual's uniqueness, they sometimes tend to inflict abuse. My daughter is special and gifted, and I had to learn that not everyone was going to understand that. To be honest, I was a little apprehensive to enroll my daughter in this school. Not that I did not trust the word of my pastor, but it was fear from everything I had already been through.

However, I was obedient and trusted God. When she started at the new school, there were some challenges but nothing like before. The staff at this school were truly people of God and did not turn their back on my daughter; instead, they prayed for her and worked with her. My daughter had been hurt and rejected so much and she was not easily trusting of others. But once she knew you cared about her, she was the absolute sweetest towards you. It took a few months, but the cycle was broken. I began to not only have peace, but I felt it. The numerous phone calls per day stopped and she felt welcomed and loved at her new school.

In December of 2018, I was promoted to Dorm Counselor Supervisor. This is where God granted me the opportunity to touch the lives of women. I did group and individual counseling with sixty girls in total.

The young ladies I worked with had such potential, they just needed guidance. For many of them, life happened, as it does for all of us. I feel honored and blessed to have had the opportunity to make an impact on all the lives God permitted. I decided that I wanted to do more. I wanted to be influential in helping people to not be stuck or lose sight of their purpose. As such, I was led by God to go into the Mental Health field and truly pursue my passion. In June 2019, I began working with clients.

My desire and heart grew quickly, and I knew that this was what I wanted to do full time. So, after eight and a half months, I resigned as Dorm Counselor Supervisor and became a full-time Mental Health Therapist.

I desired to share my story with the world for a few different reasons. My first reason is: never to allow the world to tell you or your child who they are. As a parent, always advocate for your child. Be open to guidance and advice, but make sure you are praying and using wisdom. Do not allow others to dim your child's light. My second reason is in Proverbs 3:5-6, the Word of God says, "trust in the LORD with all your heart and lean not on your own understanding; in all your ways submit to Him, and He will make your paths straight." Stop trying to figure things out on your own. Do not stray away from what you do not understand.

When I let go and let God, my circumstances changed. The devil could not hold me down anymore. I was able to get out of my bed because my depression was gone. My anxiety was gone because God gave me peace. Isaiah 54:17 says, "no weapon formed against you shall prosper, and every tongue which rises against you in judgment you shall condemn. This is the heritage of the servants of the LORD, and their righteousness is from Me," says the LORD. Know that God is with you, even in your midnight hour. Even when it seems like your circumstance is not changing, continue trusting and seeking God. I am a living witness and my story is my testimony of what God can do for you.

For all of those parents out there who can identify with my story, I want you to be encouraged and never give up on your child or God. For those of you, who identify with my career journey, trust God because you don't know where he is taking you. I decided to go into Mental Health because I want to be the person to others that I was looking for when I was going through my dark moments. My outlook on helping children is different because I know when individuals begin acting out, it is not coming from just anywhere. Things have happened, and support is needed. I believe every person God sends to me is reachable in some way. I believe God called me to make a difference and my testimony is my fuel to help those in need. Throughout this journey in my life, it has become clearer that God has destined me to be a voice of wisdom, strength, and a guiding light to others. I do not credit myself when I see individuals breaking free from depression, anxiety, torment, and grief. I give all honor, glory, and praise to God for what He instilled in me to reach others. I know I am destined by God for greatness and I continue to stand firm on His Word. I pray that I have touched someone's life and I want you all to be encouraged and blessed!

CHAPTER 6

God Wants Us to Be Unstuck

Pamela Mauzon

I can recall a time when I was stuck in the mud and dust of life. I couldn't see a path to my future for quite a while. I was back from where God had called me to be. Today, after overcoming many of his pursuits, I can confidently say, I am destined to be an overcomer and a conqueror. There is a song that says, "I can see clearly now, the rain is gone." That has been my go-to song ever since I started to see the light at the end of the tunnel. I am destined to soar like an eagle.

Destiny is assigned to my future and it is to yours as well. It's chasing us down. For me, destiny means recognizing challenges as opportunities to grow. This is the first step for growth. In other words, if God said it, I believe it, and that settles it in my life. This is why the devil can't stand my praise or yours, but he cannot stop the hand of God in our lives. When we walk in destiny, we become confident in the fact that "no weapon that is formed shall prosper." The devil cannot have anything that is connected to the child of God. I'm fearless in this destined race. After you have overcome the type of challenges that I have encountered, it is easy to become fearful; and that was once a part of my life. Thank God, I have mustered up the boldness, courage, and confidence to press forward knowing no matter how hard the task is I have learned to trust God. I would like to share with those who are trapped or stuck in situations that seem unfixable or facing challenges that feel like there's no means of escape, that there is a way out.

You must trust God to deliver you, and once God delivers you from the bondage, you are no longer bound. You are free and will become fearless. Don't you know that who the Son sets free is free indeed? It's a good feeling to be free, so pause for a minute and thank Him for what He delivered you from, and to what service he is purposing you. God has not given you the spirit of fear but of power, love, and a sound mind. As I've gotten older, I have gotten wiser. I have been seeking the Lord more and living for Him. I yielded myself to the Spirit of God, but I have realized that things are not always easy on the Lord's side. There are many avenues that I have to tackle in prayer, in order to bind up and loose, to live this fearless life. I had to learn to take everything, and I mean EVERYTHING to the Lord in prayer and to allow Him to fight my battles. I also had to walk in the authority of Jesus Christ to let the devil know that I'm not scared. I won and got the victory over fear.

The Bible says that we must cast our cares upon Him for He cares for us. God will sustain you for He is the Keeper of your soul. Continue the journey even amidst your fearful state. Don't worry, God will bring you out. I kept holding on to the horn of the altar and I wouldn't let go and you will have to do the same. Living confidently is believing that you can be all that you say you are. The Scripture says we will have what we say. So that makes me who Christ says that I am, and I say to you today, "YOU CAN MAKE IT WITH THE LORD ON YOUR SIDE." I'm walking in the authority of Jesus Christ and learning to lean and depend on my Savior. That is the Master's plan. I'm preparing myself in this everyday walk with Christ to win and stay strong. Listen, God commissions us to fight some battles and sometimes He wants us to be silent.

A part of my testimony is that I used to get pushed around a lot and suffered name-calling to the point where I felt as if I didn't know how to defend myself. I relied on the Word of God, which says, "Vengeance is mine, I will repay." Yes; my Advocate, my Lawyer, my Mouthpiece, lets me know that once I have a God, those who seek to fight me will stumble. Perfect love casts out fear. Fear is a stronghold used by the prince of the air to conquer us. Jesus has given us spiritual tools with which we are able to fight; we should utilize our weapon which is the sword of the Spirit. The truth of the matter is that the enemy is an accuser of the brethren so he will always find something to make us fearful of. The devil is a deceiver.

CHAPTER 7

Chosen for Destiny

I'm chosen! Yes, I can truly say that I'm chosen. Being chosen is a serious task. Let's look at some chosen Bible characters such as: Joseph, Leah, and Jesus. But what does it mean to be the chosen one? It simply means knowing that you are destined for greater things. If you were to look at yourself in the mirror, what would you see? You'll see your reflection looking back at you. It is a reminder that you were chosen for greatness. Greatness doesn't just happen overnight. This seed was planted in the womb! That's right. When I was in my mother's womb, there was a call on my life. I had no idea until I became older and came in the full acknowledgment of what was going on. This is Purpose.

The Bible states that "many are called but few are chosen." I am chosen to serve, love, and care for others. Growing up, I never understood my gifts. Many times, the enemy fought me because of my gift. Now I know how Joseph felt being hated. Being chosen means there is great potential in you. People may try to get into your head to change your thoughts about your destiny. It's ok. You are where God wants you to be. It's ok to be different They're not going to understand or get you anyway. Even if they consider you to be crazy, guess what? They are not telling a lie. The truth of the matter is that you are spiritually crazy for Christ. Being chosen also means being set aside from this world, to be used for the Master's will, so don't try to fit in.

When I was a little girl about ten years old, I was outside playing one day. I remembered as plain as day, how a girl, bigger than I, came in the middle of the road wanting to fight me because of something that she heard. I didn't know what was going on. I prayed and prayed until I prayed myself out of the fight. Jesus heard my prayer and rescued me. In the year 1990, I gave my life over to the Lord and was seeking Him for the Holy Ghost. In 1992, I received the gift of the Holy Ghost. This was in Greensboro, North Carolina. Even though things were out of control, Jesus' hands were still on my life. I never thought for a moment to give up or throw in the towel. The Holy Ghost gave me the grace to keep on running the race. When you are destined, you are determined! Like Joseph, you may be picked on, but look at his end; he went from the pit to the palace, from being hated for his dreams to him interpreting the King's dreams. Dream smashers and dream killers are waiting to see you fall or die. Hold strong to your faith and know that greater is He that is in you than he that is in the world.

CHAPTER 8

Get Back in The Game

Never consider yourself to be a failure, even if life takes you for a loop and things happen to make you feel bad. I have heard these words many times, "I can't, I tried, or I failed," but these words do not define you. Go ahead and get back in the game, you have nothing to lose, but everything to gain, once you jump back in with your trust being only in God. Like you, so many times, I tripped and failed, but God was in the midst of my mistakes; He kept me.

Tell yourself every day that you've got this, you can achieve this. Don't you dare give up when your dreams are waiting for you in your future. That's what makes it worth fighting for. Look at the story of David and his encounter with Goliath the giant. What are your Goliaths? You can win. David was a little boy, and his confidence made him take out a giant. What can you do as an adult? When the Philistine was weakened, God gave David the strength of an army. God used the foolish things to confound the wise.

Where it was impossible to kill a giant, God made it possible for David to take one stone and a slingshot to defeat him. That's all God! If you stay in the game, you too will get to the place where you can say "I can do all things through Christ who strengthens me." Keep fighting to keep the faith, position yourself in the battle, guard your Spirit with only good thoughts, and then let this mind be in you, which was also in Christ Jesus. Do not believe anything the devil says about you, because the devil is a liar and the truth is not in him. He is the father of all lies. Anything he says is coming from the pit of hell to make it appear as if you are unable to run this destined Christian race or be a good team player. Listen, he is not the coach. He cannot disqualify you or take you out of the game. He does not have the first or last say over your life.

God's grace is sufficient for you. He's your biggest Coach, your biggest Fan. Jesus says that He will never leave you nor forsake you; He will be with you even until the end of the world. That is a guarantee. So come on, jump back in, and get back in the game because you are not a failure.

You may be down right now, sick in body, suffering from low self-esteem, encountering financial problems, or feeling like you are in the miry clay, I'm urging you to fight. I am counting on you; like our Heavenly Father is depending on you. You're a winner, you are destined.

I remember a special lady who was so dear to me in my life until God called her home. She was my dear mother, Tracy. She was a stalwart in the Faith; she always had a kind word of wisdom to say to someone who was going through a situation, despite how she felt. She kept the faith to fight for victory although her health was a challenge and people were unfair to her. She was kicked around, lied on, misused, and talked about. She didn't stand down, she fought to win in prayer, as Paul mentioned in 1 Timothy 6:12, "fight the good fight of the faith." Many witnessed that she was destined for greatness. Let's talk about the cloud of witnesses. Ofttimes we have witnesses to see us fail but God also helps us with a cloud of witnesses to see us win. See yourself as a winner.

This is a true story. I was speaking to a young man before he became a teacher, he didn't go to college right away. After graduating from school, he took a job making less money than he previously earned. Knowing that this wasn't for him, he asked his mom, "Mom, do you think that I have the chance of going to college to get my degree?" The answer to his question was "yes." So, he got back in the game to pursue further education. When you are destined, never aim low, but see yourself as an eagle. Do you remember the song "I believe I can fly?" Best believe you can touch the sky by faith.

I CAN'T BE STOPPED

As I close out my section, I'm determined in this destined race to reach the goals that are set before me to achieve. I know that I'm capable of doing it because of Who holds my future, which is Jesus Christ. Therefore, I will not let anything, or anyone get in the way of my blessings! In this season and time, I'm running full force. I remember when I had no voice to speak at all; I was voiceless and had shortness of breath. If I wanted to scream, it was very painful to scream and to speak.

There were times when I was unable to swallow. I started decreeing and declaring things that must change in my life, and they did. My Pastor, Bishop James Rogers, preached on this message one Sunday morning. He declared that what God has for me is for me. Once you know your purpose, keep running, you just have to do it. This reminds me of the biblical story in which Jesus attended a wedding and they ran out of wine. The mother of Jesus spoke and said, "whatever He said, just do it."

Too many times, we hesitate when it's time to just do it. I have been tested in this area many times. I remember once there was a revival going on at a church in Pompano Beach, Florida, and the Lord put a pressing in my Spirit to go to this revival. While getting ready to go to church, my auntie and some other family members came over to visit me with my mom. They tried everything in their power to keep me from going to that revival that night. However, I didn't let them stop me because I felt a blessing was about to come my way. Sure enough, the revivalist called me out and spoke a word into my life concerning me and my unborn child. I was so glad that I was determined to push the spirit of distraction out of my way.

SCRIPTURES TO REMEMBER

Isaiah 54:17 - "No weapon formed against me shall prosper and every tongue that rises against me in judgment thou shalt condemn for this is the Heritage and the servant of the Lord and righteousness is of me," says the Lord.

2 Corinthians 10:13 - "We, however, will not boast beyond proper limits but will confine our boasting to the sphere of service God himself has assigned to us, a sphere that also includes you."

I John 4:4 - "Greater is He that's in me than he that is in the world."

1Timothy 6:12 - "Fight the good faith. Lay hold on eternal life, whereunto thou art also called and hast professed a good profession before many witnesses."

1 Peter3:9 - "Be not weary in well-doing."

2 Timothy 4:7 - "I have fought a good fight, I have finished my course, I have kept the faith."

Footnote:

"Dear Soldier, keep on fighting; you will win. You've got this; run until the end of your race. Remember nothing is over in life until God says so. The torch is in your hand, run with it."

CHAPTER 9

Liberation

The Power of Words for The Destined Woman

Andrea Paler

I have always expressed my true essence more thoroughly through poems. They allow a variation of writing and creative expressions. Take the time to read below. I hope you are inspired.

Liberation

My voice was endless in the dark sky,

reaching for stars that never shine.

As tears embrace my soul,

my body awakens with fear

not to ever witness a love

filled with affection.

Oh, my children, shall I

pass this unwanted passage,

Telling the world that my life

is a whirlwind of lies?

Woman cry out your afflictions.

Let no other tie you down.

Build a strong wall and nestle your babies.

Stand Strong...Stand Strong.

Stand Strong.

This poem I call, 'Liberation', as it depicts for me the words my mother Marta, ignited in me as a child. She often would say in her broken English and a Puerto Rican accent, "Don't let anyone, man or woman, take your voice away, as you are God's child." I must say it had more significance to me coming from her native language of Spanish. Nevertheless, for me as a 7-year-old, her words did not have great importance until many years later.

Marta was a powerful, strong woman both in size and heart; however, her joyous love for life ceased temporarily in the arms of my father Cheo, an alcoholic schizophrenic, who was 16 years her senior. The image of my father dragging my mother's long black hair and body down a flight of stairs, and the whimpering noise coming from her mouth, yelling his name to stop as every inch of her body ached, is an image that never left me. I witnessed all this as our neighbor tried to shovel my siblings and me into her adjoining apartment. I managed to break away from her arms and stood in shock until my father looked up and saw my face in tears and released his grip from my mother's hair and left her there on the steps as he left the building.

My father left our home and went to live with his siblings for a short time and returned unapologetically. I never knew what he did to change his negative behavior as my mother never spoke about it. To date, I don't know if he went into a drug rehabilitation program or a psychiatric treatment center. I only knew that my father was a changed man, no more drinking or smoking. He still drank his beers, but fewer and fewer. After a while, there were no more altercations between him and my mother. A transformation occurred after my father became melancholic, and my mother found inner strength, became the head of the household, and many times, took on the role of both mother and father. I believe her transformation was my initiation into becoming a strong woman of faith; as she would often say, "I could not raise you without God's help." However, that image of my father having control over my mother still reverberates in my mind and as I matured into an adolescent and then a young adult, these feelings filled my heart with mistrust and even hatred towards men.

As a young child, I struggled with these images in my head and often believed that this was the way a wife and mother were to be treated. Where was God, the One that I knew was in my parents' home, the One the Catholic Church talked about, and the One for whom the Pentecostal woman would profess her love for on a Saturday morning? She would afterwards indulge in a homemade bowl of chicken soup and Italian bread my father made for her, as part of our family's appreciation. Where was her God when my mother was being beaten by the love of her life? This was my life's focus; to regain that control, and to never have a child ever witness that ugliness. How could a loving father do this to his children, be so brutal to the wife he promised to love and obey?

Once again where was God and how had He not protected my mother and her children? The question was also, "How could a woman liberate herself from this ordeal?" According to the Merriam Webster dictionary, the word 'liberation' is defined as "the act or process of freeing someone or something from another's control." That day I vowed that before anyone takes control of me, I will take control of my life. Throughout my early childhood years, my focus was not so much on finding the answer to my question, where was my God, but more so to be a strong woman with the only thing I had, which was my education, and my love for God; a love so powerful, I could not describe. To forget the memories of that dreadful day, I tried to liberate myself through education and by being the best woman that I could be. Both my parents were invested in education and they would state these words to their children, "In this world you have three things in life, and they are, God, Family, and Education." These words were instilled in me, and became my motto, as both my parents never let me forget them.

Education was important to both my parents, as neither held a college degree. My father completed the sixth grade and started working at age 12 to provide for his siblings and father after his mother died when he was 8 years old. However, my mother completed high school and obtained a nursing certificate. Amazingly, in my eyes, they were the most educated persons I knew, as they both helped me with my academics and gave me the best advice. School was my escape from the outside world, so I excelled in the only thing I knew - academics. By the time I was 12 years old, I was accepted into an advanced program and completed the 7th and 8th grades concurrently.

This was an accomplishment for me as my goal was to be the best student, and at the same time, I kept wondering where my God was. A year later, my parents told me, their eldest child, that they were separating and that my father was going to live somewhere else. I blamed myself for their separation, even though both said their separation had nothing to do with me. Once again, where was my God? Why couldn't He keep them together? I realized I was part of the statistics - another child who came from a broken home.

At age 14, I decided to find God and attend church more regularly, sometimes twice in one week; I also volunteered to tutor and read the scriptures at the church services on Sundays. My life was so vested in the church that when I failed to attend, my week felt unfulfilled. Being part of the church was an intricate part of my family upbringing. As an existing part of my life, I spent most of my leisure time helping the priests and nuns run the after-school program while mentoring other youths in reading and writing. My church became the place at which I was nurtured into becoming a loyal follower of our Lord Jesus Christ. My love for Jesus was so powerful that I made a decision to become a nun and made preparations to apply, after which I was accepted into an all-woman Catholic College run by Maryknoll sisters.

At age 17, I attended Marymount College in Tarrytown, New York where my education incorporated Christian teachings with a major in Psychology. At Marymount College, my goal was to understand the teachings of Jesus Christ and to find my answer as to where I fit in Jesus' teachings. My time at Marymount was a challenge as I was an average student trying to master the sciences and soon discovered that I excelled in the Humanities, Psychology, Education, and Sociology. However, the most challenging experience that I had to face was being accepted in a predominantly Caucasian college, at which I was one of six minority women: four African Americans and two Puerto Ricans. The minorities who were accepted in the past came from low socioeconomic backgrounds and big cities; therefore, back in 1976, I did not meet the approval of most of the other Caucasian female students.

These young women came from upper socioeconomic backgrounds from the 50 states and overseas, e.g., Spain, Ireland, and Venezuela. This was reflected in the looks I received when I entered the cafeteria. I never noticed the stares I received until another student pointed it out as we sat in the same eating areas, and she said, "Are you in a state of denial? Look how they stared at us!" "Why?" I asked. She said, "because they are not given the same financial assistance and scholarships that we get as we are poor but have potential." My schoolmate explained that there was jealousy, and the expectation from our estranged classmates was that as the minority group, we were not going to succeed and graduate from college.

I never imagined this to be normal, that another classmate's jealousy would be mine to be concerned about, and therefore, I made a sound decision to make friends no matter their economic standing. I purposely forgot what my classmate said, as I soon realized that she had a political and prejudiced stance to keep the bridge from being built to accommodate communication between students of different cultures, races, and socioeconomic backgrounds. My mind kept focusing, not on our differences, but on our similarities; we believed in one common identity, our belief in God and His son, Jesus Christ. I managed to graduate from college in 1980 but struggled to get into a graduate program due to not having the expected grade point average; I returned home.

With determination and prayer, I knew that somehow, I would get into a graduate program as I believed in myself. My mother kept saying I could stay in New York, but there was a sense of urgency that I felt. I had to travel, as my dreams were taking me to other places that did not look like a home, and in one particular dream, I saw letters and buildings. I was able to remember the letters of my dream and wrote them down and unscrambled them, spelling the state of Connecticut and one additional letter "W." After searching in the library for universities in Connecticut. I found Wesleyan University and spoke to the dean of Psychology, who said I could take non-matriculated classes.

I took his advice as a green light to get on a greyhound bus from New York and traveled to Middletown, Connecticut. Looking back now on how I blindly did things, is hilarious, I was not even sure I'd be admitted to the school. I did not set up an appointment with a professor or chairperson, I didn't even have a place to stay overnight if I needed it; I realized I just took a great big leap of faith. God's presence was with me nevertheless; He surrounded me. It was a miracle when I met with the chairperson of the Psychology department; he accepted me into two of his advanced undergraduate classes. Our Lord Jesus Christ led me again, and as I was waiting to register, a female student befriended me. She was amazed that I had traveled from New York to Connecticut, a six-hour bus ride to be exact, just to register for two classes and didn't even have a place to stay and no financial aid to pay the tuition. The student offered me a cot to sleep overnight at her place with her other roommates so that I could attend one of the classes that were starting the next day. That night I lay on the cot in amazement and thanked God for the kindness these young ladies had shown me.

The next day was filled with more joy and appreciation, as God showed me the signs that I needed to stay in Connecticut After my first class ended for the day, my professor began speaking to me about a special graduate program for students wanting to be teachers. He informed me that he had mentioned my name to the dean, and that the dean wanted to meet me. Once again, without thinking, I ran to the new department and asked to speak to the dean. On meeting the dean, I shared with him my desire of wanting to obtain a graduate degree in Education and Psychology. He attempted to convince me into returning to New York and recommended another university so that I would not have to commute; he also expressed concern that I would not be able to begin graduate work due to my not having the grade point average required for the program. However, my persuasion and

LIBERATION

perseverance persisted, and he mentioned that he could not explain it, but he saw something in me, and that characteristic was determination. He gave me a one-semester trial period after which I was again given the green light to take three classes. Surprisingly enough, I was offered a financial aid package geared toward minorities, and of course, I took full advantage of it. After the semester, I did some graduate work and met the standard.

    I was also able to move into graduate housing and meet other female students who shared a big home. Our Lord was not finished with me as my life was going to change once again, and I would meet people that would be my pathway to His throne. During the last year of my graduate program, one of my roommates asked me to live with her because her boyfriend was traveling. Our friendship soon became strong, this was my first introduction to living with an individual who suffered from mental health issues. My new roommate Jewel explained to me that she suffered from 'bipolar disorder.' There were times she was very sad and other times when she would be manic. My experience with my roommate led me to visit her in a psychiatric hospital in which she was voluntarily admitted for stabilization. I was her roommate for one year until she and her fiancé decided to get married and buy a home. I then had to rent a room, 20 minutes from the university.

    As I traveled by bus to keep an appointment with a landlord who wanted to rent me a room, I got lost and ended up at the wrong location. Instead of waiting for the next bus, something inside me told me to wander off into the first residential area I saw. It felt as if my body was being led and I had no sense of fear within me. As I wandered off, I saw a little boy, who looked as if he was about 5 years old with wide brown eyes, black hair, and olive skin staring from a window. I took his presence as a sign that maybe his parents could give me directions and I could call the landlord as I did not have a cell phone. As I walked to his home, the boy yelled in Spanish to his mother that a woman was approaching their door. After knocking on the door, a woman in her early thirties with hazel eyes and brown hair opened the door and in Spanish asked me what I wanted. I told her I desired to use her phone as I was searching for an address and got lost.

After explaining who I was and the reason for wanting a room to rent, this woman, whom I will call Carmen, said her two young children ages five and seven each had their bedrooms, but usually slept together as her son was scared to sleep alone. To my amazement, she said she had wanted to rent the room, showed me the bedroom, and told me that the rent included all amenities including home-cooked meals. Of course, I took her offer and called the landlord who was waiting on me and explained that I had received another offer. Carmen called her husband, who came from work and met me. It was agreed that she would transport my belongings the next day.

Once again, I was destined to meet this couple and their children. Within the year, I had established a wonderful friendship with this family and even had experience living with another individual who suffered from another severe mental health disorder called Schizophrenia. Carmen's husband, whom I will call Jim, was experiencing irrational thinking, auditory hallucinations, and at times, was paranoid. Our relationship was respectful and at times even therapeutic, as he would invite me to attend his medication management appointments with him and his psychiatrist. Unbeknownst to me, this was another indicator that my life was headed in the direction to help individuals with mental health challenges.

My experience at Wesleyan University played an essential part in obtaining a teaching degree. Unfortunately, after two years into the academic program, my mother became ill and I had to return to New York without initiating my dissertation. I had to leave my friends and forestall the progress I had made. Coming home had its sad and joyous moments, as I was glad to be with my mother, but was disappointed in having to place my dissertation on hold. My time at home was occupied with aiding my mother back to health as she had undergone major surgery. Once she recovered, my focus was on resuming my dissertation. With the supervision of a college professor, I was able to successfully defend my dissertation at Hunter College in New York.

My dissertation was completed in 24 months as I was allowed during that time to teach at the college as part of my dissertation process. After graduation, I was able to obtain a teaching job in a daycare center at the kindergarten level but never expected my life to change once again. As a teacher in a daycare center, my job was to make certain that the children were safe, happy, and educated. I never dreamt that my time would also be spent investigating children's home environments, an experience that would pique my interest in the Social Services arena.

During the first year of teaching, I encountered a four-year-old boy, whom I will call Mark. He was taller and heavier than his classmates and he came from a single-parent home and had no siblings. I noticed Mark's interaction with the other children was aggressive, and at times, his communication skills only incorporated the words, "leave me alone," "No," and "I hate you." There were rare moments where I, or the assistant teacher in the classroom, would see Mark smile or get along with the other children as he had the reputation of being the class bully. His negative conduct continued for months, even after using behavior modification interventions where he was rewarded for his good behavior and would appropriately interact with his peers. However, his good conduct was often short-lived, and he reverted to his aggressive behavior.

On one occasion, everything that was questioned about him came to be understood. Mark was observed in the playroom taking the clothes off a girl doll and pushing a block inside the private parts of the doll in a very forceful manner. It so happened that the assistant teacher saw this behavior and alerted me, and I witnessed it. What I witnessed was an aggressive four-year boy doing something of which he should have had no knowledge, and this was a red flag that something was wrong at home. After asking his mother if anything had changed at home, she mentioned nothing had changed at home, and that she was living with her boyfriend and son. For Mark's safety, the Department of Special Services for Children in the state of New York was contacted, and after their investigation, it was concluded that Mark had been molested by his mother's boyfriend. Mark's mother's boyfriend was prosecuted, and the child's mother followed through with her son's mental health recovery and his anger subsided in the classroom. This unfortunate experience for Mark sparked in me an interest in the possibility that there could be other 'Marks' in this world who were being physically and emotionally harmed. This experience led me to work for the Special Services for Children and Families Division in New York City.

Once again, I was destined, as God was calling me to do different works and touch other people's lives. I worked for two years in the Special Services for Children and Families Division and unfortunately removed many children from their parents' care due to neglect and abuse. This was heartbreaking but essential for the safety of the children, and at the same time, it was my introduction to working with troubled families and children. Whenever I had to remove a child or children from a parent's care, I did so in a respectful manner, and also explained the process for reuniting them with their children. There were many times I left the parent's home without an incident. I believe that when I spoke, God was speaking through me.

God also placed me on the path to return children to their parents and guardians. I was able to monitor many of the parents' progress, and they were able to meet the criteria of the Special Services Department reunification process. However, others were not, and this was most heartbreaking as these parents lost their parental rights. My journey did not stop there and after two years of working in Special Services for Children and Families, I landed a job working in a shelter for homeless men. This was my first supervisory position, and with this experience, I knew that my goal was to continue working in Social Services. Again, I knew God wanted me to learn the skills essential to communicate with others and to alter the image I held of homeless men, whom I assumed were in that plight because they did not want to work. I quickly learned that this was far from the truth. I experienced a real awakening that these men's afflictions were due to have been in situations of war, family separation, suffering from mental and/or physical illness, and loss of employment. I soon realized that none of these men ever wanted to be homeless.

From this gradual journey of working with the homeless, God's path led me to oversee an 86-bed supported housing program in New York City where I supervised mental health professionals; I also monitored male and female clients diagnosed with co-occurring disorders including psychosocial illnesses and substance abuse. In this position, I was able to use my psychology and educational background to guide and empower both the staff and clients we served. However, in reality, the most profound discovery I made with this new job was my interest in how clients became diagnosed, and what led them to be homeless, unstable, unemployed, under-educated, disconnected from family and friends, and lacking a belief in God.

Surprisingly, I thought that persons who suffered from mental illness had no belief in Jesus Christ or practiced their faith. However, after speaking with these individuals, I soon realized that my image was superficial, as almost every individual in the program believed in Jesus Christ and would start their day in prayer and appreciation for residing in a program with people who welcomed them despite their afflictions.

Throughout my years of employment in the housing program, my ultimate goal was to once again understand that our Lord Jesus Christ was planning my future. I learned how to better understand the mental health illness my father experienced and how to forgive him for the times he had alcoholic blackouts and beat my mother. I had a better understanding of the days he would go missing and we all worried about his safety; or the times he went on drinking binges and took all the life insurance policies and surrendered them to enjoy his luxurious lifestyle.

The more I invested my time working with these wonderful individuals, the more I realized they were just like my father and I was destined as an adult to teach them the coping skills to manage and improve their lives - something that was impossible for me to achieve with my father as a child. Many of my colleagues and staff recognized how well I connected with psychiatric clients and staff who were in recovery and also working with co-occurring clients. My accomplishments did not go unrecognized by the agency's CEO and director, who recommended I pursue a degree in Social Work.

With their approval, I applied to two Social Work schools in New York and was accepted to both but chose Hunter College School of Social Work for its history and devotion to working with the homeless population and its affordable tuition. However, after two and a half years of taking evening classes and working full time at the supported housing program, I achieved another master's degree in 1995. Unfortunately, I could not share this success with my mother as she passed away unexpectedly in 1989 at the age of 51. My father had retired several years earlier and was thrilled that I had another degree and that it focused on working with individuals with co-occurring disorders. He felt this was my way of accepting that he had an uncontrollable illness.

My father died four years later at age 77 from a heart attack in his favorite chair in my sister's home. He had overcome his drinking problem 30 years prior and never manifested another psychiatric symptom after he had stopped drinking. I was so proud of him and his accomplishments, as he became a poster person in his community, and was known as the one who was sober and would often give advice both on life-skills and spiritual guidance to other alcoholics and those in recovery. I found this out from his neighbors after he had died. His friends said, "Your father was a blessed man, as he would never turn his back on others and often had time for a 'listen and a talk' when asked."

When I looked back on my journey of finding out where my God was and why he had me witness domestic violence as a young child, I now realize where he was taking me. He was preparing me to work with hurt children, individuals with mental illnesses, and those with substance abuse issues; it was already imprinted in my childhood that this was a path I had to endure. The players on this path were first: my father, with his alcoholic traits and behaviors, secondly, my first graduate school roommate, Jewel, who befriended me and asked me to visit her in a psychiatric ward, after having suffered bouts of depression and manic behavior; thirdly, was the family from whom I rented living space and whose schizophrenic father would ask me to accompany him to his many medication management appointments; fourth, were the men in the homeless shelter who were frequently turned away by several community members; and finally, yet importantly, are the many South Florida families that I currently serve, and to whom I deliver guidance and offer options and resources conducive to a healthier and more productive quality of life.

They were, and have become, the voice from God letting me know that our Lord Jesus never left me, as, with each step and experience I encountered, He was there teaching me along the way. He is the answer to my liberation, to free the afflicted of mental illnesses, and to finally accept my childhood past. I believe and continue to believe that I was destined for this profession by God Himself, and I love Him dearly for this life.

RESILIENCE

>My eyes were bestowed upon you;
>Listening to your heartbeat,
>I trusted that the love we shared
>would be forever.
>Pondering the joys and cries
>of our children.
>Wishing that our future would lead to years together.
>One small indiscretion,
>One small misunderstanding
>Led to the separation of our lives, children, and home.
>The words 'we' and 'us'
>became 'him and her.'
>Words of affection replaced
>With anger and resentment.
>Role models for our children,
>Now have become strangers to them.
>Asking children to choose mom or dad brings

inconsistency and uncertainty.

You must be resilient, as with change, comes acceptance.

And with acceptance, comes our love for each other.

I called this poem 'Resilience' as that is the goal to be reached by the parents and children that undergo divorce and separation. What does it mean to be resilient? I will share this quote from one of the parents from my program. She said, "Resilience is a choice, a vow, a promise to endure what breaks us down. A fire that no one will be allowed to put out, for it is stroked with love. The knowledge that nothing is ever fully lost, no matter how far we stray. It is two hands that hold on no matter the storm." In my profession as a social worker, I work with divorced and cohabiting individuals who have decided to end their relationship after having children. They have to endure the process of the family court system. This is before getting a final divorce and/or an established time-sharing agreement for visitation of their children. There are many other types of divorce proceedings that do not involve the family court services; however, those cases are far and few.

In this chapter, I share my experience working with parents who need to co-parent but are challenged with their emotions and frustration towards each other due to the end of their relationship. These parents are offered strategies to change their emotions towards each other and are reminded of their union as man and wife and their acceptance with God. It may be difficult to accept, but even in these unpleasant situations, they are destined. The co-parenting process is very dear to me as I came from loving parents who after 13 years of marriage, legally separated, but never divorced.

This cycle was repeated in my life, as after 7 years of marriage, I found myself filing for divorce and separating our children ages 4 and 8 months old from their father. This resulted from cultural and religious differences; futuristic goals made it also challenging to stay together. This was a decision that was made without proper guidance from a pastor, priest, rabbi, or marriage counselor. Somehow, if these individuals were contacted, maybe there would have been a greater chance of the marriage continuing. My goal was not to separate our children from their father, although that is what he believed when I relocated from New York to Florida back in 1998.

My former husband knew where we lived, had communication with the children, and had flexible visitations timesharing, where we would both travel with the children to each other's home state. We didn't have to undergo the referral process of attending co-parenting sessions with a mental health therapist. I must attribute our civil relationship to our respect for each other and open communication skills. However, parents' civility is not common amongst some of today's parents, and therefore, many parents and other guardians have to participate in co-parenting sessions when they disagree and need guidance from a mental health worker to come to a civil agreement. The timeframe of co-parenting sessions is at the discretion of the therapist and the participants.

As I worked with co-parenting clients, I realized that God had destined me to be part of their lives and He used me as a vehicle to change their negative way of thinking towards one another. In addition to assisting them to see the goodness in each other, I got to show them how they both shared the same love for their children. My experience in dealing with co-parents is that there is no one formula or strategy to implement, and it's a combination of my personal experience with an emphasis on promoting change, reflection, and acceptance on how God can transform lives. Therefore, I implemented steps that could be a helpful tool to engage a conversation between individuals having challenges. Challenges such as experiencing divorce or separation, timesharing with children, frustration and anger at the other parent, and family court services bureaucracy were attacked with these steps.

As a therapist for many years, I realized that to get individuals to communicate, one must make it entertaining, humorous, and practical, as this will capture a person's interest. Therefore, I implemented what I called 'God's Recipe' for a successful and progressive co-parenting system. In God's recipe what you will find are ingredients of love displayed in this formula:

Step 1 - Obtain a pair of parents or guardians, i.e. aunt, uncle, grandmother, grandfather, etc.

Step 2 - Add some scripture such as:

> Ephesians 4:2-3 - *With all humility and gentleness, with patience, one another in love, eager to maintain the unity of the Spirit in the bond of peace.*
>
> 1 Corinthians 13:4-5 - *Love is patient, love is kind. It does not envy, it does not boast, it is not proud. It does not dishonor others; it is not self-seeking. It is not easily angered; it keeps no record of wrongs.*

1 Corinthians 16: 14 - *Do everything in love.*

1 Corinthians 13: 13 - *And now these three remain; faith, hope, and love. But the greatest of these is love.*

1 John 4:12 - *No one has ever seen God, but if we love one another, God lives in us, and His love is made complete in us.*

Step 3 - Place them inside an area full of bedded flowers, i.e. rose petals, carnations, any aromatic scents appealing to each of them.

Step 4 - Ask each participant to drop their favorite scripture into a pot.

Step 5 - Let it sit, don't mix, let the ingredients blend. Let it stand for 10 minutes.

Step 6 - Ask each participant to reach into the pot and reach inside and select a scripture, read, and reflect on how it relates to their current situation.

Step 7 - Repeat step 6 until each participant has related two scriptures.

God's recipe worked. It was utilized in the following cases with great results and for client confidentiality, names have been changed. My clients Mary and Sebastian could not agree on how to raise their boys, but with the introduction to God's Recipe, they were able to appreciate each other's views on how their children should be raised. They completed the co-parenting sessions earlier than expected and now have joint custody of their two boys Frank and Lindsay. The couple was now able to effectively communicate with each other, and with the re-introduction of God's scripture, they could visualize how their faith in God influenced their 23 years of marriage. They were receptive to co-parenting sessions and were able to be encouraged to have additional sessions with their pastor to address past marital issues. Sebastian received pastoral individual counseling and this collaboration was successful; they renewed their vows and remarried, and now all two children live with them.

Maria and Milagros were both faithful Christians who found much-needed forgiveness from each other. Maria suffered from mental illness and Milagros recognized that Maria had completed all her psychiatric treatment services and that it was important for her children to get consistent love from their mother, which meant they would live with her. Maria was given permanent physical custody and she scheduled bi-weekend visits with Milagros.

One of the most powerful ingredients that our Lord God provides us with, is his love, and with love, you can be resilient and bounce back from any challenging position in your life. Working with individuals who have to endure divorce or separation and then have other persons make decisions to have their children separated from a loving home, is devastating. I thank God for allowing me to work with parents who have had to undergo this traumatic experience and for guiding me in finding creative ways to introduce His scriptures and extending helping hands to these individuals. I am truly destined to be a representation of our God.

CHAPTER 10

Sis Accept Who You Are!

Ashley Sylveste

She is looking in the mirror, but who or what is she looking for? That's a question she wishes she could answer...but she cannot. For as long as she could remember, she has asked herself these same questions. However, no one could tell that every day she questioned her existence. From the time she would wake up, until the time she would go to sleep, she felt that she was a mistake. They had already prejudged her. Everyone, from her family and friends, had already categorized her. They never even asked or tried to get to know her. They judged her from the many masks she would learn to wear, and as she got older, she improved at changing these masks. When she was younger, they saw a little girl with a lighter-skinned complexion, and assumed she was conceited and hated persons of darker hues. But truthfully, she wished she was darker, as having such features, she would not feel so different and maybe could fit in a little more. As she got older, some of the people closest to her began to see that she was somewhat funny. They just thought she was goofy, and that she wasn't quite intelligent. They couldn't see that it was a disguise she used to just try to fit in, or that it was a cry for help. She was lost and empty.

When she entered middle and high school, they began to say, "Oh, she thinks she's bad", or, "She thinks she's cute." If only they truly knew. Who was she? She was a girl who struggled with suicidal thoughts as long as she could remember. She was a girl who had given up on the will to live even before she knew what living was. She had given up on herself even before she knew who she was. She couldn't see what everyone else saw, when they looked at her, even though she wished she could. Then just maybe she wouldn't struggle with herself or hate herself as much as she did. Because no matter what they saw, when she looked in the mirror, she saw someone completely different. She saw someone ugly with pimples and a huge gap that had been handed down like a family inheritance - worthless and unable to be loved. As she grew older, things continued to change for the worse. Her sense of purpose grew even less, and she began to rebel even more. All this started at the place in which she spent most of her time...at church.

She promised herself that when she became an adult, she would never step back into a church. Everyone at church seemed to be going through hell as well. She even convinced herself that she didn't believe in love. Why should she? The one person from whom she ever really wanted or ever needed love, was busy wanting love herself. By trying to fill the void created by her father after he left home, she began to entertain the belief that she had been put in this world in error. Why would God put her here to feel such emptiness and hopelessness? Growing up in the church, she had always heard that God doesn't make mistakes. They used to say that even if you don't know what and why, He allows certain situations to happen; just believe that there is a reason behind it.

She was unaware that persons who are truly called by God, must endure several trials and tribulations. However, in those trials and tribulations, you begin to learn about the gifts God has given you, and most importantly, you begin to build a deeper connection with Him; with every trial that you endure, He brings you out victoriously.

One day she ended up in jail because she had gotten in trouble with a few of her friends. She ended up being locked up for seventeen days and on her first day in, she was put in with the general population. On a certain occasion at which some detainees were being released, a lady walked up to her and whispered in her ear to pick a certain program. She had no idea who this lady was and what she was talking about.

Later that day, an officer passed out some papers with three abbreviations on it. She remembered what the lady whispered in her ear and checked the box. The next day another officer came in and said, "Most of y'all are going to have to stay in the general population because the program most of you requested is full."

Then he said, "There's only room for one person." From a list of twenty persons, this young lady was the only person chosen, and she had no idea what she had signed up for. She eventually learned that she had signed up for a Christian program. They had church three times a day where pastors and other Christians would come in, talk with them, and give testimonies on how God had delivered them and set them free.

While she was in there, she often spoke with a certain young lady named Deb who had been in jail for two and a half months and still hadn't gotten a court date. Deb told her that she had two young boys and their favorite holiday was the Fourth of July, which happened to be 5 days away at the time. One night she had a dream and the following morning she shared it with Deb. She explained to her how she saw her walking through the jailhouse doors and waving goodbye. Of course, Deb didn't believe it because she had just spoken with the clerk of courts who informed her it could take up to six months to get a court date. But she explained to Deb that God could do the impossible if she had a little faith. Two days later she woke up to find a letter on her bunk from Deb, expressing her thanks. I truly believe God is good. Deb got released on time served. So even in bad situations, God always gets the glory.

Deb got to see God move and even though she had to suffer in jail, she learned to endure. Romans 5:3-4, "More than that, we rejoice in our suffering, knowing that suffering produces endurance, and endurance produces character, and character produces hope." I was 'SHE' who shared that word with Deb. Growing up, struggling with self- acceptance, not knowing who or what I was meant to be, not knowing my purpose or feeling unworthy. I was scared of embracing new challenges out of a fear of failure; that was a part of the old 'SHE' who no longer lives in me. I realized that everything that I experienced, was designed for me to endure. 1 Corinthians 10:13, "There hath no temptation taken you but such that is common to man: but God is faithful, who will never suffer you to be tempted above that ye are able; but will with the temptation make also the way of escape, that ye may be able to endure."

Too often, we hear people say, "He won't give us more than we can bear." The devil would always fill my mind with certain negative thoughts that urged me to end my life, because he knew the call that God had placed on my life. He wanted to end my life before I knew just how blessed and chosen by God I was. From the womb, I was destined for greatness. I was scheduled, appointed, and ordained for this walk. I learned that I may never be known for being a singer, dancer, model, or even an actress (which was a dream of mine). I may never speak in large crowds or appear on a television show. Those things were not what He had in mind when He chose me. Those pieces were not in my puzzle box to make me a whole picture.

I had to have suicidal moments so that my heart could relate to someone else who was having those same thoughts. I had to feel unworthy so I could tell someone just how special God thinks they are. I had to feel ugly and have low self-esteem so that when a little girl is struggling, trying to find her beauty based on what the world says, I can tell her that God did not make a mistake when He made you. 2 Corinthian 1:3- 4, "Blessed be the God and the Father of our Lord Jesus Christ, the Father of our mercies and God of all comfort, who comforts us in all our afflictions, so that we may be able to comfort those who are in any affliction, with the comfort with which we ourselves are comforted by God." I had to learn that everyone's path is different. Growing up and being raised in the church, I always knew about pastors, preachers, teachers, ministers, deacons, and prophets. I was told that God had blessed me with a gift and not to run from it. Truthfully, it was something I always ran away from.

As a young girl, I never wanted a title, I just wanted to go to church and sit down and hide away. If I had to have a title, it would be the usher, but I always knew I was different. From a young child, I could remember meeting people for the first time and just having overwhelming feelings of sadness and anguish that would sweep over me. I couldn't explain it. It would sometimes take me days to shake those feelings. At that time, I didn't know what it was, and truthfully, I hated the emotion. But as I got a little older, I was told that God had blessed me with a unique gift and that I should not to run away from it. Whatever!!! I just wanted to blend in with my peers and engage in similar activities. However, because of my unique spiritual gift, I was never inclined to respond in anger towards anyone for a long period, no matter what occurred between us.

A conviction would kick in immediately and that made me angry as I didn't always like being the one who cared. I would sometimes question God; I asked Him why, but never aloud. Why do they get to ill-treat me without caring? Or why do I have to be the prophetess who only sees the bad stuff? However, I learned to appreciate everything He showed me, even when I did not understand it. My co-pastor always told me to be happy about the things He showed me because I could help someone correct their life. At around the age of 6 years old, I told my mom I dreamt that I was hit by a car and the dream surely came through. My mom had told me not to ride my bike until she came home. But as an anxious child, I couldn't wait. I didn't listen, so I asked my aunt if I could ride it. As my mom was driving back home at a speed that was slower than her normal speed of driving, unsuspectingly, I came around neighbor's the driveway into the road and boom, I was hit. My mom stopped and quickly jumped out of the car. I was on the ground; I was not hurt; however, my mom was shaken but relieved that I was okay.

Because of my disobedience, my dream came to pass. This Destined Walk is not easy, but it is worth it. Our Father is always with us and He doesn't take our trials and struggles for granted, especially when we are doing his Kingdom's work. 1 Peter 5:10 - "But the God of grace, who hath called us unto His eternal glory by Christ Jesus, after that ye have suffered a while, make you perfect, establish, strengthen, settle you." I always heard that no matter how far you try to run from God and do your own thing, He always finds a way to pull you back in. That is so true when I reflect on some of the situations that I have been through in my life. It's like being in a puppet show. When children watch a puppet show, they are in awe because they believe that the puppets are real and able to do their own thing. That's us when we try to run away from God and do our own thing. We are being naive like little children.

For a while, He will even let us do whatever it is that we want to do before He pulls us back in; he allows certain things to take place. You see, a puppeteer manipulates the puppet to get it to do what he wants it to do. And no... God does not manipulate us, but He has control over our lives. Just when we start to think we can do it by ourselves or we are on the verge of killing ourselves, He steps in and his entry is always on time. For instance, when I was in jail and a few of the inmates would stand and give their testimonies, I would be amazed when they thanked God for allowing them to be in jail. I never understood that at the time. I was locked up for thinking I was big and bad, but most of these females were facing major charges and battling even bigger addictions.

On one particular day, this lady truly simplified it and made me understand why they were grateful to be in jail. She started by saying, "The first time I went to jail, I was 16, and the last time I had been to jail I was 42." That immediately caught my attention. She went on to say that she was addicted to crack and heroin for half of her life. Now at 54 years old, she has been clean for 12 years. She said that every time she went to jail, she believed it was God saving her from overdosing. The last time she ever did drugs, she said she was in a crack house and as she was doing drugs, she began to talk to God, asking Him to please let something happen because if it didn't, she knew she would die from an overdose that night. She said within 20 minutes the house was raided and she never touched drugs again. It wasn't easy but she feared she wouldn't have made it back again.

God hears our prayers even when we think He doesn't. I often felt as though God didn't hear my prayers or didn't care enough to answer me. I had to learn that God doesn't answer our prayers the way we want Him to do, but He answers our prayers according to our needs. He does not just hear our prayers, but also our questions and the matters of our heart. He can use people or things, and sometimes, He uses the people or things that we least expected to answer or give confirmation for questions our hearts seek. He used the burning bush to get Moses' attention in Exodus 3, or the talking donkey in Numbers 22:28. I remember one day my heart was heavy and I was questioning God concerning some issues. I had told God I wanted Him to speak through someone at church that Sunday, as that would be the confirmation. I needed to make my decision. However, God is in control and He doesn't do things when, where, and how we want. Sunday came and I was excited because I knew I was going to get my answer. However, I did not get an answer. While attending to an errand a couple of days later, I overheard some people talking, and during their conversation, I got the answer to the issue that was troubling me. I had wanted it answered at church so I could use the excuse that they already knew a bit of what was going on, but He had to use two people I didn't know to answer my question. Sometimes God will even use you to give yourself confirmation or a word.

I often would ask myself, "Why me". Now I the question is, "Why not me." Being Destined is a walk. You cannot make it a race. Sometimes you may even have to skip, jump, or crawl to that place where He wants to take you. It is an ongoing process and with processes, there are steps you must take to make it to the next level. Everyone's process will not be the same, but it should produce similar results such as changes within yourself, a deeper relationship with Him, and the ability to be impactful.

Philippians 1:6 – 'Being confident of this very thing, that He has begun a good work in you and will perform it until the day of Jesus Christ.'

What are some ways in which you struggle to accept who God created you to be?

Write four things you like about yourself:

For every negative thing, there is a positive, why not focus on the positive and pray about the negative? Can you do that?

Write a 3-line love letter to yourself:

What does John 3:16 say?

Know that if no one else loves you, God does, and you were destined to be here!

www.ingramcontent.com/pod-product-compliance
Lightning Source LLC
Chambersburg PA
CBHW031159160426
43193CB00008B/432